Table Of Contents

Introduction to Zoho Creator Low Code Guide for Beginners

What is Zoho Creator?

Zoho Creator is a cloud-based low-code development platform that allows users to create custom applications for their businesses with ease. It is designed to help organizations streamline their processes and increase productivity by automating various tasks.

With Zoho Creator, users can create applications for a wide range of purposes, including project management, inventory management, customer relationship management, and more. The platform provides a drag-and-drop interface that allows users to design and build their applications without the need for coding knowledge. This makes it an ideal tool for businesses that want to create custom applications but don't have the resources to hire a dedicated development team.

Zoho Creator also comes with a range of built-in features and integrations that make it easy to create powerful applications. These include features such as workflow management, reporting and analytics, and data visualization tools. Additionally, the platform integrates seamlessly with other Zoho products, such as Zoho CRM and Zoho Books, making it easy to create a complete business solution.

One of the key benefits of Zoho Creator is its flexibility. Users can create applications that are tailored to their specific needs, and the platform can be customized to match the branding and design of their business. This means that businesses can create applications that are unique and reflect their own identity, rather than relying on generic solutions that don't meet their needs.

In addition, Zoho Creator is a cost-effective solution for businesses of all sizes. The platform offers a range of pricing plans, from free plans for small businesses to enterprise-level plans for larger organizations. This means that businesses can choose the plan that best fits their needs and budget, without having to worry about expensive upfront costs.

Overall, Zoho Creator is a powerful and flexible low-code development platform that can help businesses streamline their processes and increase productivity. Its ease of use, built-in features, and affordable pricing make it an ideal solution for businesses looking to create custom applications without the need for coding expertise.

Why use Zoho Creator?

In today's fast-paced business world, companies are looking for ways to streamline their operations and improve efficiency. One of the ways they are doing this is by adopting low-code platforms like Zoho Creator. Zoho Creator is a powerful tool that allows businesses to create custom applications without the need for extensive coding knowledge. In this chapter, we will explore why Zoho Creator is an excellent choice for businesses of all sizes.

1. Easy to Use

Zoho Creator is designed with the end-user in mind. The intuitive drag-and-drop interface makes it easy for anyone to create custom applications. You don't need to be a programmer or have any coding knowledge to get started with Zoho Creator. The platform also offers a wide range of templates that you can use to create your applications quickly.

2. Customizable

Zoho Creator is highly customizable, allowing you to tailor your applications to your specific business needs. You can add custom fields, create workflows, and automate tasks to streamline your business processes. The platform also offers a wide range of integrations with other Zoho apps and third-party tools, making it easy to connect your applications with other systems.

3. Cost-Effective

One of the biggest advantages of using Zoho Creator is its affordability. Unlike traditional custom software development, you don't need to spend a fortune to create custom applications with Zoho Creator. The platform offers flexible pricing plans that cater to businesses of all sizes, making it an ideal choice for startups and small businesses.

4. Scalable

Zoho Creator is a scalable platform that can grow with your business. As your business expands, you can add more features and functionality to your applications. The platform can handle large volumes of data, making it suitable for businesses with complex data management needs.

In conclusion, Zoho Creator is an excellent choice for businesses that want to streamline their operations and improve efficiency. The platform is easy to use, customizable, cost-effective, and scalable, making it an ideal choice for businesses of all sizes. If you are looking for a low-code platform that can help you create custom applications quickly and easily, Zoho Creator is the perfect choice.

Who is this book for?

Who is this book for?

This book is for anyone who is interested in learning about Zoho Creator Low Code development. If you are a beginner in the field of low-code development, this book is the perfect guide to get started with Zoho Creator. The book is designed to be a step-by-step approach to help beginners understand the basics of low-code development and how to use Zoho Creator to build applications.

If you are a business owner or a manager looking to streamline your business processes, this book is for you. Zoho Creator is a powerful tool that can help you build custom applications to automate your business processes. With this book, you will learn how to build applications that can help you manage your inventory, sales, customer relationships, and more.

If you are a student or a developer looking to expand your skills, this book is for you. Zoho Creator is a low-code platform that can help you build applications quickly and efficiently. You don't need to be an expert in programming to use Zoho Creator. With this book, you will learn how to build applications using visual tools and drag-and-drop interfaces.

If you are a Zoho user, this book is for you. Zoho Creator is part of the Zoho suite of applications. If you are already using Zoho applications like Zoho CRM, Zoho Books, or Zoho Projects, you can use Zoho Creator to build custom applications that integrate with your existing Zoho applications. This book will help you learn how to build custom applications that can help you get the most out of your Zoho suite of applications.

In summary, this book is for anyone who is interested in low-code development and wants to learn how to use Zoho Creator to build custom applications. Whether you are a business owner, a manager, a student, or a developer, this book is the perfect guide to get started with Zoho Creator.

What can you expect to learn from this book?

If you are a beginner to Zoho Creator Low Code and looking to learn how to build apps quickly and efficiently, this book is the perfect guide for you. The Zoho Creator Low Code Guide for Beginners: A Step-by-Step Approach has been designed to help you learn how to create custom apps and automate business processes without any programming skills or technical knowledge.

In this book, you will learn how to use Zoho Creator to build customized web and mobile applications for a variety of industries such as finance, healthcare, education, and more. You will also learn how to automate your business processes, manage your data, and integrate with third-party applications.

The book starts by introducing you to the basics of Zoho Creator Low Code and its interface. You will learn how to navigate the platform and create your first application. The book then takes you through the process of designing your app, adding fields, customizing forms, and creating workflows.

You will also learn how to manage your data effectively, including how to create reports, charts, and dashboards. The book covers advanced topics such as integrating with third-party applications, creating custom functions, and configuring APIs.

By the end of this book, you will have a thorough understanding of Zoho Creator Low Code and how to use it to build custom applications for your business. You will be able to automate your business processes, manage your data, and integrate with other applications to streamline your workflows.

Overall, this book is an excellent resource for beginners who want to learn Zoho Creator Low Code and build custom applications quickly and efficiently. With its step-by-step approach, it is easy to follow and will help you become a proficient app builder in no time.

Getting Started with Zoho Creator

Creating your account

Creating your account

Before you can start using Zoho Creator, you need to create an account. This process is quick and easy, and you can get started in just a few minutes. Here's how to create your account:

Step 1: Go to the Zoho Creator website

The first step is to visit the Zoho Creator website. You can do this by typing "Zoho Creator" into your web browser, or by clicking on the link provided in the book. Once you're on the website, click on the "Sign up for free" button.

Step 2: Create your account

Next, you'll need to create your account. This involves entering your email address, choosing a password, and selecting your country and time zone. You'll also need to read and agree to the terms of service and privacy policy.

Step 3: Verify your email address

After you've created your account, Zoho Creator will send you an email with a verification link. Click on the link to verify your email address and activate your account.

Step 4: Choose your plan

Once your account is activated, you'll need to choose your plan. Zoho Creator offers a range of plans to suit different needs and budgets. You can choose a free plan, or upgrade to a paid plan for additional features and functionality.

Step 5: Start using Zoho Creator

With your account set up and your plan selected, you're ready to start using Zoho Creator. You can access the platform from your web browser, or by downloading the mobile app for iOS or Android.

In summary, creating your Zoho Creator account is a simple process that can be completed in just a few minutes. By following these steps, you'll be on your way to creating custom applications and automating your business processes with ease.

Navigating the interface

Navigating the Interface

Zoho Creator is a powerful low-code platform that allows users to create custom applications without writing any code. However, the interface can be intimidating for beginners who are just starting to explore this tool. In this chapter, we'll provide you with a step-by-step guide on how to navigate the interface and get started with Zoho Creator.

First, let's take a look at the main dashboard. When you log in to your Zoho Creator account, you'll see a list of all your applications. If you're just starting out, you'll have an empty dashboard. To create a new application, click on the "Create New Application" button.

Once you've created an application, you'll be taken to the application builder interface. This is where you'll design your application and add your data. The interface consists of three main areas: the left-hand sidebar, the center workspace, and the right-hand sidebar.

The left-hand sidebar contains all the components you can add to your application. These include forms, reports, pages, and workflows. To add a component to your application, simply drag and drop it from the sidebar to the workspace.

The center workspace is where you'll design your application. This is where you'll add fields to your forms, design your reports, and create workflows. The workspace is divided into two main areas: the design area and the data area. The design area is where you'll design the layout of your forms and reports, while the data area is where you'll add your data.

The right-hand sidebar contains all the settings and properties for your application. This is where you'll configure your fields, set up your workflows, and manage your data. The sidebar is divided into several tabs, including the Fields tab, the Reports tab, and the Workflows tab.

As you can see, the Zoho Creator interface can seem overwhelming at first. However, with a little practice, you'll become familiar with the various components and be able to create custom applications with ease.

In the next chapter, we'll dive deeper into the different components of Zoho Creator and show you how to create your first application.

Understanding the basics of low code development

Low code development is a method of software development that involves using a visual interface and pre-built components to create applications. Low code development is becoming more popular because it allows developers to create applications faster and with less coding knowledge. Zoho Creator is a low code development platform that allows users to create applications without needing to know how to code.

Low code development is based on the concept of abstraction. Abstraction is the process of hiding complexity and focusing on the essential aspects of an application. In low code development, developers use a visual interface to create applications by dragging and dropping pre-built components. These components could be anything from a button or a form to a database or an API.

Low code development platforms like Zoho Creator use a visual interface to create applications that are easy to use and maintain. The visual interface makes it easy to create applications without needing to know how to code. Zoho Creator also provides a library of pre-built components that can be used to create applications quickly.

Low code development is ideal for businesses that need to create applications quickly and with minimal coding knowledge. It is also ideal for businesses that need to maintain and update their applications frequently. Low code development platforms like Zoho Creator provide a way for businesses to create applications that are easy to use and maintain.

In conclusion, low code development is a method of software development that involves using a visual interface and pre-built components to create applications. Zoho Creator is a low code development platform that allows users to create applications without needing to know how to code. Low code development is becoming more popular because it allows developers to create applications faster and with less coding knowledge. It is ideal for businesses that need to create applications quickly and with minimal coding knowledge.

Building Your First Zoho Creator Application

Creating a new application

Creating a new application in Zoho Creator is a straightforward process that can be done in just a few simple steps. Before you begin, it's important to have a clear idea of what you want your application to accomplish and what features it should include.

To create a new application, log in to your Zoho Creator account and click on the "New Application" button located in the top right corner of the screen. This will open up a new window where you can select from a variety of application templates or start from scratch.

If you choose to start from scratch, you'll be prompted to set up your application's database by defining the fields you want to include. This can be done easily by clicking on the "Add Field" button and selecting the appropriate data type for each field.

Once you've set up your database, you can begin designing your application's user interface. This can be done using Zoho Creator's drag-and-drop interface builder, which makes it easy to add and arrange different elements like forms, tables, and buttons.

Next, you'll need to define your application's workflow by setting up rules and triggers that dictate how data is processed and how different actions are triggered. This can be done using Zoho Creator's visual scripting tool, which allows you to create complex workflows without needing to write any code.

Finally, you can customize your application's look and feel by choosing a theme and adding your own branding elements. Once you're satisfied with your application, you can publish it for others to use by clicking on the "Publish" button.

Overall, creating a new application in Zoho Creator is a simple and intuitive process that doesn't require any coding experience. With its powerful features and user-friendly interface, Zoho Creator is the perfect platform for anyone looking to create custom business applications quickly and easily.

Adding fields and forms

Adding fields and forms is one of the most important steps in building an effective application in Zoho Creator. In this chapter, we will explore the various types of fields and forms available in Zoho Creator and how to use them to create an efficient application.

To start with, fields are essentially the building blocks of your application. They allow you to collect and store data in a structured manner. Zoho Creator offers a wide range of field types, including text, number, date, time, and many others. Each field type comes with its own set of properties and validation rules, which you can customize based on your specific needs.

To add a new field, simply click on the "Add Field" button in the Form Builder and select the field type you want to add. You can then enter the label, name, and other properties for the field, and save it to your form.

Once you have added all the required fields to your form, you can start designing the form layout. Zoho Creator offers a drag-and-drop interface that makes it easy to arrange fields in the desired order and format. You can also customize the appearance of the form by selecting different themes, colors, and fonts.

In addition to the basic fields, Zoho Creator also offers advanced field types such as lookup fields, formula fields, and file upload fields. These fields allow you to create more complex forms that can perform calculations, display related data from other forms, and upload files such as images and documents.

Finally, Zoho Creator also provides a variety of form templates that you can use as a starting point for your own applications. These templates include pre-built forms and fields that you can customize to fit your specific needs.

In conclusion, adding fields and forms is a crucial step in building an effective application in Zoho Creator. By using the various field types and form templates available, you can create a customized application that meets your specific business needs. With its intuitive interface and powerful features, Zoho Creator makes it easy for beginners to create professional-grade applications without any coding skills.

Setting up workflows and approvals

Setting up workflows and approvals is an essential aspect of any business process. In Zoho Creator, you can easily automate your workflows and approvals using the drag-and-drop interface. Workflows are a series of tasks that are performed in a specific order, while approvals are the process of obtaining authorization for a specific action or decision.

To set up workflows and approvals in Zoho Creator, you need to follow these steps:

1. Identify the process: The first step is to identify the process that needs to be automated. You can create a flowchart or a process diagram to visualize the process.

2. Create a form: Once you have identified the process, you need to create a form that captures the necessary data. You can use the drag-and-drop interface to create the form and add the necessary fields.

3. Create a workflow: After creating the form, you can create a workflow that defines the sequence of tasks that need to be performed. You can use the workflow builder to create the workflow and add the necessary actions.

4. Create an approval process: Once the workflow is created, you can add an approval process to the workflow. The approval process defines the approval hierarchy and the criteria for approving or rejecting a request.

5. Test the workflow and approval process: After creating the workflow and approval process, you need to test it to ensure that it works as expected. You can test the workflow and approval process by submitting test data and verifying the results.

In conclusion, setting up workflows and approvals in Zoho Creator is a simple and straightforward process. By automating your workflows and approvals, you can save time, reduce errors, and improve efficiency in your business processes. With the drag-and-drop interface and the workflow builder, you can create workflows and approvals without any coding knowledge.

Customizing the user interface

Customizing the user interface is an essential aspect of creating an effective application. With Zoho Creator, you have the ability to customize every aspect of your user interface to create a unique, user-friendly experience. In this chapter, we will explore the different ways you can customize the user interface to improve the usability of your application.

One of the first things you will want to do when customizing your user interface is to create a theme that reflects your brand. Zoho Creator provides a number of built-in themes that you can use as a starting point, or you can create your own custom theme. You can change the colors, fonts, and styles to create a cohesive look and feel for your application.

Another way to customize your user interface is by adding widgets. Widgets are pre-built components that you can add to your application to provide additional functionality. For example, you can add a calendar widget to your application to allow users to schedule appointments or events. There are a variety of widgets available in Zoho Creator, including charts, maps, and forms.

You can also customize the layout of your application by using the drag-and-drop interface. This allows you to rearrange the elements on the page to create a more intuitive user experience. You can move fields, buttons, and other elements around the page to make it easier for users to find what they are looking for.

Finally, you can customize your user interface by adding custom scripts. Zoho Creator uses Deluge, a powerful scripting language, to allow you to add custom functionality to your application. For example, you can add validation scripts to ensure that users enter data correctly, or you can add workflow scripts to automate certain tasks.

In conclusion, customizing the user interface is an important part of creating an effective application. With Zoho Creator, you have the flexibility to create a unique, user-friendly experience that reflects your brand and meets the needs of your users. Whether you are adding widgets, customizing the layout, or adding custom scripts, you can create a powerful application that will help you achieve your business goals.

Advanced Features of Zoho Creator

Integrating with other Zoho apps

Integrating with other Zoho apps

One of the best features of Zoho Creator is its seamless integration with other Zoho apps. This means that you can easily connect your Zoho Creator app with other Zoho apps like Zoho CRM, Zoho Books, and Zoho Invoice, to name a few. With this integration, you can streamline your business processes and make your work more efficient.

Zoho Creator has a built-in integration module that makes it easy to connect with other Zoho apps. To start integrating, you need to first navigate to the "Integrations" tab in your Zoho Creator app. From there, you can select the Zoho app that you want to connect with and follow the on-screen instructions.

For example, if you want to integrate your Zoho Creator app with Zoho CRM, you can do so by selecting "Zoho CRM" from the list of integrations. You will then be prompted to enter your Zoho CRM credentials and authorize the integration. Once the integration is complete, you can start syncing data between your Zoho Creator app and Zoho CRM.

Another great feature of Zoho Creator's integration module is that you can create custom integrations using Zoho's APIs. This means that you can connect your Zoho Creator app with other third-party apps and services that are not part of the Zoho ecosystem.

To create a custom integration, you need to first obtain the API key for the app or service that you want to connect with. You can then use Zoho Creator's built-in API module to create a connection between your app and the third-party service. Once the connection is established, you can start syncing data between the two services.

In conclusion, integrating with other Zoho apps is a powerful feature of Zoho Creator that can help you streamline your business processes and make your work more efficient. Whether you want to connect with other Zoho apps or third-party services, Zoho Creator's integration module makes it easy to do so.

Creating reports and dashboards

Creating reports and dashboards is an essential aspect of using Zoho Creator to its fullest potential. Reports and dashboards provide valuable insights into data, making it easier to make informed decisions, identify trends, and track progress. In this subchapter, we will explore how to create reports and dashboards in Zoho Creator.

Reports are a way to summarize data from different tables or forms in Zoho Creator. Reports can be customized to show only the information that is relevant to the user, and they can be shared with others. Reports can be created by navigating to the "Reports" section of Zoho Creator and clicking "New Report." From there, users can select the table or form they want to create a report for and choose the fields they want to include in the report. The report can also be filtered and sorted to display the data in a specific way.

Dashboards, on the other hand, are a collection of reports that provide a high-level view of data. Dashboards can be created by selecting the "Dashboards" section of Zoho Creator and clicking "New Dashboard." Users can then choose the reports they want to include in the dashboard and arrange them in a way that makes sense. Dashboards can also be customized with widgets and charts to provide a visual representation of the data.

One of the best things about Zoho Creator is that reports and dashboards can be shared with others. Users can choose to share a report or dashboard with specific individuals or groups, or they can make it public for anyone to view. Reports and dashboards can also be scheduled to run automatically, so users can receive the information they need without having to manually run the report or dashboard.

In conclusion, creating reports and dashboards is an essential aspect of using Zoho Creator to its fullest potential. Reports and dashboards provide valuable insights into data, making it easier to make informed decisions, identify trends, and track progress. With Zoho Creator, users can create customized reports and dashboards that can be shared with others and even scheduled to run automatically. With these tools, users can take their data analysis to the next level and make better decisions for their business.

Using Deluge, the Zoho Creator scripting language

Zoho Creator is a powerful low-code platform that allows users to create custom applications with ease. One of the standout features of Zoho Creator is its scripting language, Deluge. Deluge is a simple yet powerful scripting language that allows users to add custom logic and automate workflows within their applications.

If you are new to Zoho Creator, Deluge may seem intimidating at first. However, with a little guidance, you can quickly learn to use Deluge and take your Zoho Creator applications to the next level.

The first step in using Deluge is to understand its syntax. Deluge is a simple scripting language that uses a combination of keywords, variables, and functions to perform specific tasks. Deluge scripts are typically written in the "Script" section of a Zoho Creator application.

One of the most powerful features of Deluge is its ability to interact with data in Zoho Creator. Deluge allows you to perform a wide range of data manipulation tasks, such as filtering, sorting, and updating records. You can also use Deluge to create custom forms and reports, automate workflows, and even integrate with external applications.

To get started with Deluge, it's important to have a clear understanding of your application's requirements. This will help you identify the specific tasks that you need to automate or customize using Deluge. Once you have a clear understanding of your requirements, you can begin writing Deluge scripts to accomplish these tasks.

There are many resources available to help you learn Deluge, including online tutorials, documentation, and community forums. Zoho Creator also offers a range of pre-built applications and templates that you can use as a starting point for your own applications.

In conclusion, Deluge is a powerful scripting language that can help you take your Zoho Creator applications to the next level. With a little guidance and practice, you can quickly learn to use Deluge to automate workflows, customize forms and reports, and interact with data in Zoho Creator.

Automating tasks with APIs and webhooks

One of the most significant benefits of using Zoho Creator is its ability to automate routine tasks through APIs and webhooks. APIs, or application programming interfaces, allow different software systems to communicate with each other, while webhooks are automated messages that are sent from one system to another when certain events occur. By using these two tools, users can save time and improve their workflows by automating tasks that would otherwise require manual intervention.

For example, let's say you have a form on your website that collects customer information. You can use an API to send that information directly to Zoho Creator, where it can be stored and processed. This eliminates the need for someone to manually input the data into Zoho Creator, saving time and reducing the risk of errors.

Another example is using webhooks to automate email notifications. Let's say you have a form on your website that collects leads. Instead of manually sending an email to your sales team every time a new lead is added, you can set up a webhook that automatically sends an email to the sales team when a new lead is added to Zoho Creator. This ensures that your sales team is notified in real-time, giving them an edge in following up with potential customers.

Automating tasks with APIs and webhooks can also help you to integrate Zoho Creator with other software systems. For example, you can use APIs to connect Zoho Creator with your accounting software, allowing you to automatically generate invoices and track payments. You can also use webhooks to integrate Zoho Creator with your project management software, keeping everyone on the same page and ensuring that tasks are completed on time.

In conclusion, automating tasks with APIs and webhooks is a powerful tool that can help you to save time, reduce errors, and improve your workflows. By using Zoho Creator's built-in APIs and webhooks, you can automate routine tasks and integrate Zoho Creator with other software systems, creating a seamless workflow that maximizes efficiency and productivity.

Best Practices for Zoho Creator Development

Keeping your code organized and maintainable

Keeping your code organized and maintainable is an essential part of any software development process, including low code development with Zoho Creator. It is crucial to create a structure that ensures the code is easy to read, modify, and maintain. In this subchapter, we will discuss some practical tips to keep your Zoho Creator code organized and maintainable.

1. Use meaningful names for fields, forms, and reports

When naming your fields, forms, and reports, make sure to use descriptive names that accurately represent their purpose. Avoid using abbreviations or acronyms that may be confusing to other users. Meaningful names will make it easier for you and other users to understand the purpose of the component, which is critical when making modifications and updates.

2. Create a consistent naming convention

Having a consistent naming convention for your fields, forms, and reports will make it easier to organize and search for them. Decide on a naming convention that works best for your organization, and stick to it. For example, you could use a prefix to identify the type of component, such as "frm_" for forms and "fld_" for fields.

3. Use comments

Comments are an excellent way to explain the purpose of a particular section of code. Use comments to describe what the code does, why it is there, and any important details that may not be immediately apparent. Comments will make it easier for you and other users to understand the code and make modifications if necessary.

4. Group related fields and forms

Grouping related fields and forms will make it easier to locate and modify them. For example, you could group all fields related to a particular customer or product together in a section of the form. This will make it easier to find and modify the fields if you need to make changes.

5. Use templates

Zoho Creator offers many templates that you can use to create forms and reports quickly. Using templates will save you time and ensure that your components are consistent in design and structure. You can customize the template to fit your specific needs, but using a template as a starting point will make it easier to create maintainable code.

In conclusion, keeping your Zoho Creator code organized and maintainable is essential to ensure that your applications are easy to modify and update. Use meaningful names, consistent naming conventions, comments, grouping, and templates to create maintainable code that will save you time and effort in the long run.

Testing and debugging your applications

Testing and debugging your applications are essential steps in the development process. Testing helps to ensure that your application works as expected, while debugging helps to identify and fix any errors that may occur. In this chapter, we will discuss some best practices for testing and debugging your Zoho Creator low code applications.

Testing your applications

Before deploying your application, you should test it thoroughly to ensure that it works as expected. Here are some best practices for testing your Zoho Creator low code applications:

1. Test each component individually: Instead of testing the entire application at once, test each component separately. This will help you identify any errors or bugs in a specific component.

2. Use test data: Use test data to simulate different scenarios and test the application's functionality. This will help you identify any issues with data validation or input handling.

3. Test on different devices and browsers: Ensure that your application works on different devices and browsers. This will help you identify any compatibility issues.

4. Test with real users: Conduct user testing to gather feedback and identify any usability issues.

Debugging your applications

Debugging is the process of identifying and fixing errors in your application. Here are some best practices for debugging your Zoho Creator low code applications:

1. Use debugging tools: Zoho Creator provides debugging tools that can help you identify and fix errors in your application.

2. Review your code: Review your code to identify any syntax errors or logical errors.

3. Use logging: Use logging to track the flow of your application and identify any errors or bugs.

4. Test in a staging environment: Test your application in a staging environment before deploying it to production. This will help you identify any issues before they affect your users.

Conclusion

Testing and debugging are essential steps in the development process. By following these best practices, you can ensure that your Zoho Creator low code applications work as expected and are free of bugs and errors. Remember to test each component individually, use test data, test on different devices and browsers, and test with real users. When debugging your application, use debugging tools, review your code, use logging, and test in a staging environment.

Collaborating with other developers and users

Collaborating with Other Developers and Users

Collaboration is a key aspect of software development, and Zoho Creator offers several tools to help developers and users work together effectively. In this subchapter, we'll explore some of these tools and best practices for collaborating with others on Zoho Creator projects.

1. Sharing Applications

One of the most basic ways to collaborate on Zoho Creator is by sharing applications. This allows team members to access and work on the same app, regardless of their location. To share an app, click on the 'Share' button on the top right corner of the app builder screen. You can choose to share the app with specific users, groups, or everyone in your organization. You can also control the level of access each user has, such as read-only or full access.

2. Commenting and Chatting

Another way to collaborate on Zoho Creator is by using the commenting and chatting features. These tools allow team members to leave comments or messages on specific elements of an app, such as a form or a report. This makes it easy to discuss and resolve issues without having to switch between different tools or platforms. To use these features, simply click on the 'Comment' or 'Chat' icon next to the element you want to discuss.

3. Version Control

Version control is a critical aspect of collaboration, especially when multiple people are working on the same app. Zoho Creator offers a version control feature that allows you to keep track of changes made to an app over time. This feature also makes it easy to revert to a previous version if something goes wrong. To access the version control feature, go to the 'Settings' menu and click on 'Versions.'

4. User Permissions

Finally, it's important to set up user permissions carefully when collaborating on Zoho Creator projects. By default, users have full access to all elements of an app. However, you can limit access to specific elements or actions, such as editing a form or deleting records. This helps to prevent accidental or malicious changes that could affect the entire app. To set up user permissions, go to the 'Settings' menu and click on 'Users.'

In conclusion, collaborating with other developers and users is essential for successful software development. Zoho Creator offers several tools to help teams work together effectively, including sharing applications, commenting and chatting, version control, and user permissions. By using these tools and following best practices, you can ensure that your Zoho Creator projects are completed on time, within budget, and to the satisfaction of all stakeholders.

Scaling and optimizing your applications

Scaling and optimizing your applications are crucial steps to take when creating a successful Zoho Creator low code application. These steps help to ensure that your application runs smoothly, efficiently, and can handle increasing amounts of data as your business grows. In this section, we will discuss the various techniques and strategies you can use to scale and optimize your Zoho Creator low code application.

One of the first steps to take when scaling your application is to design your database schema efficiently. This involves creating a database schema that is easy to understand, scalable, and optimized for performance. You should also consider using indexes to improve the speed of your queries, especially if you have a large amount of data.

Another important technique to use when scaling your application is caching. Caching involves storing frequently accessed data in memory to reduce the number of times the database needs to be queried. This can significantly improve the performance of your application and reduce the load on your database.

When optimizing your application, you should also consider using asynchronous programming techniques. This involves breaking up long-running tasks into smaller, more manageable parts that can be processed in parallel. By doing this, you can improve the overall performance of your application and ensure that it remains responsive even when handling large amounts of data.

Finally, you should also consider using load balancing to distribute the workload across multiple servers. This can help to improve the performance and reliability of your application, especially during times of high traffic or usage.

In conclusion, scaling and optimizing your Zoho Creator low code application is essential for ensuring its success and longevity. By following the techniques and strategies outlined in this section, you can create an application that is efficient, reliable, and capable of handling increasing amounts of data as your business grows.

Common Use Cases for Zoho Creator

Creating a CRM system

Creating a CRM System

A CRM system is an essential tool for any business that wants to manage its customer interactions effectively. With a CRM system, you can track customer interactions, manage sales and marketing campaigns, and generate reports that help you make informed business decisions. In this chapter, we'll look at how to create a CRM system using Zoho Creator.

Step 1: Define Your Objectives

Before you start building your CRM system, it's important to define your objectives. What do you want to achieve with your CRM system? What are your business goals? Once you have a clear idea of what you're trying to achieve, you can start building your CRM system to meet those objectives.

Step 2: Identify Your Data Requirements

The next step is to identify your data requirements. What types of data do you need to collect and store in your CRM system? This will depend on your business objectives and the types of interactions you have with your customers. For example, you may want to store customer contact information, sales data, and marketing campaign data.

Step 3: Build Your CRM System

Now it's time to start building your CRM system using Zoho Creator. Zoho Creator is a low-code platform that makes it easy to build custom applications without any coding skills. Here are the steps to build your CRM system:

1. Create a new application in Zoho Creator and choose the CRM template.
2. Customize the fields in the template to match your data requirements.
3. Add any additional fields or forms that you need to collect data.
4. Set up workflows and automations to manage your customer interactions.
5. Customize your reports and dashboards to get insights into your customer interactions.

Step 4: Test and Refine Your System

Once you've built your CRM system, it's important to test and refine it. Test your system with a small group of users to see how it performs and identify any areas for improvement. Refine your system based on user feedback and continue to iterate until you have a system that meets your objectives.

Conclusion

Creating a CRM system using Zoho Creator is a straightforward process that can help you manage your customer interactions effectively. By defining your objectives, identifying your data requirements, building your system, and testing and refining it, you can create a CRM system that meets your business needs. With Zoho Creator, you don't need any coding skills to build a custom CRM system that works for your business.

Building a project management tool

Building a project management tool is a crucial task for any business, especially when it comes to managing multiple projects simultaneously. A project management tool helps in tracking the progress of each project, assigning tasks to team members, allocating resources, setting deadlines, and monitoring the overall performance of the project. In this subchapter, we will guide you through the process of building a project management tool using Zoho Creator Low Code.

Zoho Creator Low Code is an ideal platform for building project management tools as it provides a range of pre-built templates and modules that can be customized according to your specific requirements. The platform offers a drag-and-drop interface that allows you to create forms, reports, and dashboards without requiring any coding expertise.

To begin building your project management tool, you need to first define the scope and objectives of your project. This will help you in identifying the core features that you need to include in your tool. Once you have a clear understanding of your requirements, you can start building your project management tool using Zoho Creator Low Code.

The first step is to create a database to store all the information related to your projects. You can use the pre-built project management template in Zoho Creator Low Code or create your own custom database. Next, you need to create forms to collect data from your team members. These forms should include fields for project name, description, start date, end date, budget, and other relevant information.

Once you have created your forms, you can start building your workflows. Workflows are a sequence of steps that define the process of completing a task. In the case of a project management tool, workflows can include assigning tasks to team members, setting deadlines, and tracking the progress of each task.

Finally, you can create reports and dashboards to monitor the overall performance of your projects. Reports can be customized to show specific data points such as project progress, budget, and resource allocation. Dashboards provide a real-time view of your projects and can be used to track key performance indicators.

In conclusion, building a project management tool using Zoho Creator Low Code is a simple and efficient way to streamline your project management processes. With the platform's intuitive interface and pre-built templates, you can create a customized tool that meets your specific needs.

Developing a custom HR solution

Developing a Custom HR Solution

As businesses grow, the need for an efficient and effective HR solution becomes increasingly important. With Zoho Creator, you can create a custom HR solution tailored to your business needs. In this chapter, we will guide you through the process of developing a custom HR solution using Zoho Creator.

1. Define your HR requirements: Make a list of all the HR processes that need to be automated. This could include employee onboarding, performance management, leave management, time tracking, and more. Be specific about the data fields that are required for each process.

2. Create a database: Once you have defined your HR requirements, you can start building your HR database in Zoho Creator. This will act as the foundation for your HR solution. You can create fields for employee information such as name, email, address, job title, and more.

3. Build forms: Once you have created the database, you can start building forms that will allow users to input data. For example, you can create an employee onboarding form that captures all the necessary information such as personal information, job information, and emergency contact details.

4. Develop workflows: Once you have created forms, you can develop workflows that will automate HR processes. For example, you can create a workflow that automatically sends an email to the HR team when an employee submits a leave request form.

5. Add integrations: Zoho Creator allows you to integrate with other apps such as Zoho People, Zoho Books, and Zoho CRM. This can help streamline your HR processes even further.

6. Test and refine: Once you have built your HR solution, it is important to test it thoroughly to ensure that it works as expected. You can refine your solution based on feedback from users and make changes as necessary.

In conclusion, developing a custom HR solution using Zoho Creator is a straightforward process that can save businesses time and money. By automating HR processes, you can improve efficiency and accuracy while also improving employee satisfaction. With Zoho Creator, you can create a custom HR solution that meets the unique needs of your business.

Managing inventory and orders

Managing inventory and orders is an essential aspect of any business operation. It involves tracking stock levels, monitoring sales, and ensuring that orders are fulfilled in a timely and efficient manner. With Zoho Creator Low Code, managing inventory and orders has become more accessible and hassle-free.

One of the primary benefits of using Zoho Creator Low Code for inventory and order management is its ability to automate various processes. For instance, you can set up workflows that automatically update stock levels as orders are fulfilled, or trigger alerts when inventory levels fall below a certain threshold. This saves you time and effort, allowing you to focus on other aspects of your business.

Zoho Creator Low Code also allows you to customize your inventory and order management system to your specific needs. You can create fields for different product categories, set pricing rules, and create custom reports to track sales and inventory levels. This level of customization ensures that you have all the information you need to make informed decisions about your inventory and orders.

Another benefit of Zoho Creator Low Code for inventory and order management is its integration with other Zoho apps. For example, you can integrate your inventory and order management system with Zoho CRM to manage customer orders and sales leads in a single platform. This integration ensures that you have a complete view of your business operations, helping you to make informed decisions about your inventory and orders.

In conclusion, managing inventory and orders is essential for any business, and Zoho Creator Low Code makes it easier than ever before. With its automation, customization, and integration capabilities, you can streamline your inventory and order management processes, saving time, and improving efficiency. Whether you are a beginner or an experienced business owner, Zoho Creator Low Code is an excellent tool for managing inventory and orders.

Troubleshooting Zoho Creator Issues

Identifying common errors and issues

Identifying Common Errors and Issues

As a beginner in using Zoho Creator Low Code, it is important to know that errors and issues may occur as you create your application. These errors and issues can delay your progress and cause frustration, but they are also a learning opportunity to help you become a better app builder. In this section, we will be discussing some common errors and issues you may encounter when building your Zoho Creator Low Code application.

1. Syntax Errors

One of the most common errors in Zoho Creator Low Code is syntax errors. These errors occur when the code you have written does not follow the syntax rules of the programming language you are using. These errors can be easily spotted by the red squiggly line underneath the code. When you see this, you can hover over the code to see the error message and correct the error.

2. Data Type Errors

Another common error is data type errors, which occur when you try to assign a value of the wrong data type to a variable. For instance, if you try to assign a string value to an integer variable, you will get a data type error. To avoid data type errors, ensure that you use the correct data type when declaring your variables.

3. Database Errors

In Zoho Creator Low Code, you can use the database to store and retrieve data. However, you may encounter errors when trying to interact with the database. Some common database errors include incorrect table names, incorrect field names, and incorrect SQL syntax. To avoid database errors, double-check your table and field names and ensure that your SQL statements are correct.

4. User Interface Errors

User interface errors occur when there is an issue with the UI components of your application. For instance, if a button on your form is not working, it may be due to an error in the button's code. To avoid UI errors, ensure that you test your application thoroughly and check for any issues with the UI components.

In conclusion, identifying common errors and issues in Zoho Creator Low Code is essential, as it helps you to avoid mistakes and improve your app-building skills. By paying attention to syntax errors, data type errors, database errors, and user interface errors, you can create a robust and functional application that meets your needs.

Finding solutions and workarounds

As a beginner in the world of Zoho Creator Low Code development, it's important to understand that you may encounter various challenges along the way. However, these challenges should not discourage you from pursuing your goals. Instead, you should embrace them as opportunities to learn and grow.

In this subchapter, we will explore how to find solutions and workarounds when faced with challenges in Zoho Creator Low Code development.

Firstly, it's essential to understand the resources available to you. Zoho Creator has a vast knowledge base where you can find answers to frequently asked questions, tutorials, and step-by-step guides. You can also join the Zoho Creator community forum where you can interact with other developers and get assistance with any challenges you may be facing.

Secondly, it's important to break down the problem into smaller parts. This approach will help you to identify the root cause of the problem and come up with an effective solution. You can also try to reproduce the issue in a test environment to gain a deeper understanding of the problem.

Thirdly, consider using workarounds. Workarounds are temporary solutions that can help you to overcome a problem until a permanent solution is found. For example, if you're having trouble with a particular function, you can try using a similar function that achieves the same result.

Fourthly, consider seeking help from Zoho Creator experts. Zoho Creator has a team of experts who can provide you with personalized assistance and guidance on how to overcome any challenges you may be facing.

Lastly, don't hesitate to experiment and try new things. Zoho Creator Low Code development is a constantly evolving field, and there are always new solutions and workarounds to discover. By experimenting and trying new things, you can gain a deeper understanding of Zoho Creator and become a better developer.

In conclusion, finding solutions and workarounds in Zoho Creator Low Code development requires patience, persistence, and a willingness to learn. By utilizing the resources available to you, breaking down the problem, using workarounds, seeking help from experts, and experimenting, you can overcome any challenges and achieve your development goals.

Getting help from the Zoho Creator community and support team

Zoho Creator is a powerful low-code platform that allows users to create custom applications without the need for extensive coding knowledge. As a beginner, you may find yourself facing challenges or needing assistance while creating your application. This is where the Zoho Creator community and support team come in.

The Zoho Creator community is a great resource for beginners. It is a platform where users can share their experiences, ask questions, and get help from other users. You can join the community by signing up on the Zoho Creator website. Once you have signed up, you can access the community forum and connect with other users. The community is an active platform, and you can expect to receive responses to your queries from other users within a short time.

In addition to the community, the Zoho Creator support team is also available to assist you. The support team is made up of experts who are knowledgeable about the platform and can help you with any issues you may encounter. You can contact the support team through the Zoho Creator website or by email. The support team is available 24/7, and you can expect a prompt response to your queries.

When seeking assistance from the community or the support team, it is advisable to provide as much information as possible about the issue you are facing. This will enable the community or support team to provide a more accurate and timely solution. You should also be patient and polite when seeking assistance. Remember that the community and support team are made up of people who are volunteering their time to help others.

In conclusion, the Zoho Creator community and support team are great resources for beginners. They provide a platform where users can connect, share experiences, and get help from other users or experts. When seeking assistance, it is important to provide as much information as possible and be patient and polite. With the help of the community and support team, you can overcome any challenges you may encounter while creating your custom application.

Conclusion and Next Steps

Reviewing what you've learned

Reviewing what you've learned is an essential step in the Zoho Creator low code guide for beginners. It allows you to consolidate your learning, identify areas that need improvement, and develop a better understanding of the concepts.

As a beginner, you may have gone through several chapters that introduced you to the basics of Zoho Creator, including creating forms, reports, and workflows. You may have also learned how to integrate third-party applications, such as PayPal, Google Maps, and others. Now that you've completed these chapters, it's time to review what you've learned.

One of the best ways to review what you've learned is to practice. Create new forms, reports, and workflows using the knowledge you've gained so far. You can also try integrating different applications to see how they work with Zoho Creator. By doing this, you'll reinforce your learning and gain more confidence in your abilities.

Another way to review what you've learned is to take quizzes or tests. The Zoho Creator low code guide for beginners provides several quizzes and tests at the end of each chapter to help you assess your understanding of the concepts. Taking these quizzes and tests can help you identify areas that need improvement and also help you focus on the topics that you're weak in.

You can also review what you've learned by watching videos or attending webinars. Zoho Creator offers several video tutorials and webinars that cover different aspects of the platform. These resources can help you gain a better understanding of the concepts and also provide you with new ideas and insights.

In conclusion, reviewing what you've learned is crucial in the Zoho Creator low code guide for beginners. It helps you consolidate your learning, identify areas that need improvement, and gain more confidence in your abilities. By practicing, taking quizzes or tests, and using different resources, you can become proficient in Zoho Creator and create powerful applications with ease.

Planning your next Zoho Creator project

Before jumping into your next Zoho Creator project, it's important to have a plan in place that outlines your goals, timeline, and resources. This will ensure that your project runs smoothly and you achieve the desired results.

The first step in planning your Zoho Creator project is to define your goals. What is the purpose of your project? What problem are you trying to solve? Who is your target audience? These questions will help you determine the scope of your project and what features you need to include.

Next, you need to establish a timeline for your project. When do you want to start and finish? What milestones do you need to reach along the way? Having a clear timeline will help you stay on track and ensure that you meet your deadlines.

Once you have your goals and timeline in place, you need to consider the resources you'll need to complete your project. This includes the team members who will be involved, any software or hardware you'll need, and any other resources that may be required.

One of the biggest advantages of using Zoho Creator is that it's a low-code platform, meaning you don't need extensive programming knowledge to create custom applications. However, if you do need additional support or guidance, Zoho offers a range of resources including documentation, webinars, and customer support.

Finally, it's important to test your project before launching it. This will help identify any bugs or issues that need to be addressed before your project goes live. Zoho Creator offers a range of testing tools to help ensure that your project is running smoothly.

By following these steps, you can ensure that your next Zoho Creator project is a success. With its low-code platform and robust features, Zoho Creator is an excellent choice for beginners looking to create custom applications without extensive development experience.

Continuing your learning journey with Zoho Creator resources

Continuing your learning journey with Zoho Creator resources

As a beginner in Zoho Creator, you may have completed the basic courses and have a good understanding of the platform. However, to fully utilize the potential of Zoho Creator and become an expert, you need to continue your learning journey. Fortunately, Zoho Creator has a wealth of resources that can help you enhance your skills and knowledge.

Zoho Creator Help Center

The first and most important resource is the Zoho Creator Help Center. This is a comprehensive knowledge base that provides detailed information on how to use the platform. It includes guides, tutorials, FAQs, and troubleshooting tips. You can access the Help Center from the Zoho Creator dashboard or visit the website directly.

Zoho Creator Community

Another valuable resource is the Zoho Creator Community. This is a forum where users can ask questions, share tips, and discuss issues related to Zoho Creator. You can learn a lot from other users who have more experience with the platform. You can also contribute to the community by sharing your own knowledge and insights.

Zoho Creator Webinars

Zoho Creator regularly conducts webinars on various topics related to the platform. These webinars are free and cover a wide range of topics, from basic to advanced. You can register for upcoming webinars or watch recordings of past ones. Webinars are a great way to stay up-to-date with the latest features and best practices.

Zoho Creator Academy

Zoho Creator Academy is a paid resource that provides in-depth training on the platform. It includes courses on specific topics, such as database design, form customization, and workflow automation. The courses are designed by experts and provide hands-on experience with real-world scenarios. You can enroll in individual courses or purchase a subscription for access to the entire academy.

Conclusion

With these resources, you can continue your learning journey with Zoho Creator and become an expert in no time. Whether you prefer self-paced learning or interactive training, there is a resource for you. Take advantage of these resources and unlock the full potential of Zoho Creator.